Real Lives Real Listening

A Place I Know Well

Elementary
Student's Book

First Edition

Authentic listening for students at A2/B1 levels

Sheila Thorn

north★star
ENGLISH LANGUAGE TEACHING

The Listening Business

Real Lives, Real Listening:
A Place I Know Well
Elementary Student's Book, First edition
by Sheila Thorn

Published by North Star ELT
5 Leverndale Court, Crookston
Glasgow G53 7SJ Scotland
United Kingdom
www.northstarelt.co.uk

Publisher: Andy Cowle
Editorial services: SunCross Media LLC
Cover design: Studio April
Text design/Composition: Christopher Hanzie
Printed in Greece

ISBN: 978-1-907584-39-8   Student's Book with Audio CD

Free teacher's notes and answer keys available online at: **www.northstarelt.co.uk**

Photo Credits

All photos are from iStockphoto.com: Cover © RonTech2000; p6 man © Image Source; p6 flag © ayzek; p7 landscape © stevephotos; p19 woman © H-Gall; p19 flag © ayzek; p26 cottage © matthewleesdixon; p34 man © Suzana Profeta; p34 flag © ayzek; p36 telephone © Spauln; p39 cityscape © swedewah; p45 cyclist © francisblack; p49 flags © ayzek; p49 woman © laflor; p50 ship © Willard; p52 map © menonsstocks; p54 woman © Franck Boston; p54 flags © ayzek; p56 cake © Owen Price; p57 landscape © TaurusGuy

Contents

Teacher's notes and answer keys available online at: www.northstarelt.co.uk

Acknowledgements

Books, articles, lectures and workshops by the following people have been invaluable in helping me to develop the approach to authentic listening I have used in the *Real Lives, Real Listening* series: Gillian Brown, Ron Carter, Richard Cauldwell, John Field, Jennifer Jenkins, Tony Lynch, Mike McCarthy, Shelagh Rixon, Michael Rost, Paul Seligson, Adrian Underhill, Mary Underwood, Penny Ur and J.J. Wilson.

My grateful thanks to the following people and institutions for commenting on and piloting these materials:

Maria Sforza and Heather Wansbrough-Jones at *South Thames College, London*, Carol Butters, Sarah Dearne, Michelle Parrington and Justin Sales at *Stevenson College, Edinburgh*, Jonathan Fitch at *The Oxford English Centre*, Hazel Black and Chris Jannetta at *English for Everyone, Aberdeen*, Sasha Goldsmith at *Rands English Language Tuition*, Elizabeth Stitt at the *University of St Andrews*, Sophie Freeman, Jen McNair Wilson, John Marquis, Harriet Williams and Jo Whittick at *English in Chester*, Dariana Cristea, Beverley Gray and Keith Harris at *Loughborough College*, Catherine Marshall and Michelle Scolari at *Bellerbys College, London*, Kath Hargreaves, Julia Hudson and Eric Smith at *Embassy CES, Oxford*, Andy Wright at *Queen Mary, University of London*, Zoe Smith at *OISE Bristol*, Elizabeth Bray and Mike Powell at *Coventry College*, Joe Ferrari at *Dundee College* and Julia Isidro at *Kings Oxford*.

I am also extremely grateful to all the people who kindly allowed me to interview them for these books, particularly those for whom English is not their first language.

This book is dedicated to my father and to Jill for their constant love, support and encouragement, and to my dear friend Ian Sandison and my mentor, Jean Coles.

Introduction

Aims

The main aim of the *Real Lives, Real Listening* series is to provide busy teachers with ready-made listening materials which will effectively *train*, rather than just test, their students in listening. A parallel aim is to boost students' confidence in their listening skills by exposing them to authentic texts. A further aim is to introduce students to the grammatical structures and lexis which are typically used in spoken English.

The series reflects the latest academic theories on the process of decoding listening input and the importance of authentic listening practice in language acquisition. The series also reflects our new awareness of the huge differences between spoken and written English highlighted by recent research on spoken English corpora.

Authenticity

Unlike the listening texts typically found in coursebooks, each text in *Real Lives, Real Listening* is 100% unscripted. This means that students are exposed to the features of spoken English which they encounter outside the classroom and generally find so daunting. These features include assimilation, elision, linking, hesitations, false starts, redundancy and colloquial expressions.

The *Real Lives, Real Listening* series is carefully designed to include both native and near-fluent non-native English speakers, reflecting the fact that most of the English which is spoken these days is between non-native speakers of English.

Content

The series is at 3 levels: Elementary (A2/B1), Intermediate (B1/B2) and Advanced (C1/C2), and each level has 5 listening texts.

The first three listening texts in each level are accompanied by a wide variety of focused exercises from which the teacher can make a selection, depending on the needs of their students. The final two listening texts are for revision purposes. Here the speakers recycle, naturally, the lexis and grammatical structures found in the previous three texts. Each book contains verbatim transcripts and useful glossaries.

Extensive piloting of these materials has shown that students at all levels experience a huge sense of achievement when they find they can actually understand a native or competent non-native speaker talking at a natural speed. The *Real Lives, Real Listening* series provides them with that opportunity.

Content

This book is at Elementary Level, and is suitable for students ranging from lower to upper elementary levels. The first three main units are graded in terms of difficulty from easier to more challenging.

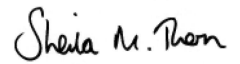

UNIT 1 Danny

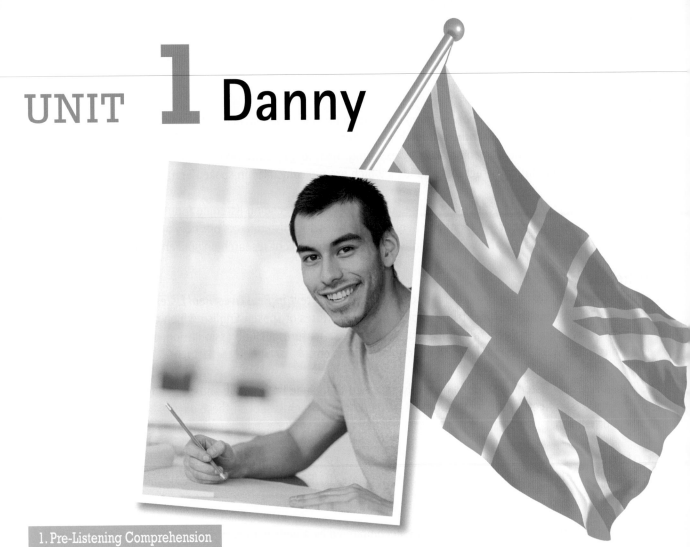

1. Pre-Listening Comprehension

Danny is a student at Nottingham University. He spent a year in Dover on a placement as part of his studies. Danny comes from a small market town near Cambridge.

Normalisation

This exercise is designed to help you get used to Danny's voice.
Tick (✓) the correct box.

1. Danny lived in Dover in his **first** ☐ **second** ☐ **third** ☐ year at university.

2. Danny says Dover is a very **small** ☐ **smelly** ☐ **sunny** ☐ place.

3. The two big ferry companies in Dover are **Sea France and B&O Ferries** ☐ **Sea France and P&O Ferries** ☐ **Sea French and P&O Ferries** ☐.

2. Listening Comprehension

Multiple Choice

Tick (✓) the correct box.

1. You can see the sights of Dover with **a tour boat** ☐ **a tour bus** ☐.

2. Danny lived in a **flat** ☐ **hostel** ☐ **hotel** ☐ in Dover.

3. He lived near **the castle** ☐ **the beach** ☐ **the cliffs** ☐.

4. Danny says the sea was **grey** ☐ **blue** ☐ **green** ☐.

5. The beach was **sandy** ☐ **stony** ☐.

6. Halfway up the White Cliffs of Dover there seem to be **trees** ☐ **caves** ☐ **cottages** ☐.

7. Danny never did a tour of Dover because **he didn't have enough time** ☐ **he didn't have enough money** ☐.

8. When Danny lived in Dover he sometimes went to **Calais** ☐ **Carlisle** ☐ **Paris** ☐.

9. Danny likes the **shops** ☐ **restaurants** ☐ **bars** ☐ in the French town.

A *used to* (do something) for past habit

The interviewer begins the interview by saying:

Now you used to live in Dover, I think?

We use *used to + infinitive* to talk about things that we did regularly in the past or states that went on for some time in the past. We often use *used to* to talk about something we did when we were younger, but that we don't do any more. Look at these examples:

'I used to walk two miles to school every day.'
'All the kids used to play in the street.'
'I used to wear trainers to work in my last job.'

B *must have been* for assumptions

When the interviewer hears that Danny's hotel was near the beach she says:

That must have been nice.

We use *must have + past participle* when we talk about something in the past which we assume was true. In this case the interviewer is sure that it was nice for Danny to stay in a hotel near the sea. Later the interviewer asks how white the White Cliffs of Dover are. Danny says:

You must have seen pictures.

In this case Danny is sure that the interviewer has, at some time in her life, seen pictures of the cliffs and therefore knows that they are really white.

C Introduction to the present perfect simple

The interviewer says:

I've never been to Dover.

This usage of the present perfect simple is very common when people are meeting for the first time and getting to know each other.

D *'cos* instead of *because* in spoken English

Both the interviewer and Danny use *'cos* instead of *because.* This is a common feature of fast spoken English.

Interviewer: *In your third year 'cos, 'cos you're a student.*
Danny: *It portrays that it is nice, 'cos you have the tour bus that goes round to see the sights of Dover.*

E The glottal stop

The glottal stop occurs when the speaker constricts his or her throat and blocks the air stream completely. This results in the speaker not pronouncing fully the –*t* sound at the end of words such as *got* or *lot*, or the –*t*– sounds in words such as *bottle* or *kettle*. This is a common feature of many British accents, and is used particularly by younger people. Notice how Danny uses a glottal stop in the following excerpts:

no<u>t</u> a <u>lot</u> of people   *I never <u>got</u> a chance*

*It portrays **tha<u>t</u> i<u>t</u>** is nice.*   *It was **quite** expensive.*

***Bu<u>t</u>** it was a nice view.*   ***Didn't ge<u>t</u>** any further than Calais.*

*very **whi<u>te</u>***

F Falling intonation for statements

In British English the voice generally falls at the end of the statement. This signals that the speaker has finished making a point. It also signals that the other person can now say something without fear of interrupting the speaker. Listen to Danny making the following statements and pay attention to where his voice begins to fall:

It's mainly just a harbour town

The sea's surprisingly blue, for England.

You must have seen pictures.

They are really white.

I never did the tour.

I never got a chance.

Didn't get any further than Calais.

G Simplification

When we speak quickly a process known as 'simplification' occurs. The speaker cuts corners and doesn't articulate words clearly. This makes it difficult for you to recognise words even if you know them already. Listen to the following words in isolation:

comfortable   *supposed*

How has the pronunciation of these words changed in a stream of speech?

So it wasn't too <u>comfortable</u>.

But Calais's <u>supposed</u> to be a nice place.

A Linking

Linking occurs when the end of one word runs_into the start_of the next word. It is very common in informal spoken English, but less so in more formal English, such as speeches or lectures.

The most common linking occurs between the letter *-s* at the end of a word when the next word begins with a vowel, as in these excerpts from the interview:

> Third year **was_in** Dover.
> But it **was_a** nice view.

However, linking also occurs with other sounds. Mark where linking occurs in these excerpts from the interview.

1. Can you tell me a bit about the town?
2. two big main companies: Sea France and P&O ferries
3. that's about it
4. The sea's surprisingly blue, for England.
5. But that's about all you can do . . .
6. There are parts of it that are nice.
7. Has it got a beach there?
8. Which is a bonus.

Now read these phrases and sentences aloud and remember to link words.

B Hearing the sounds of English 1

Listen and repeat each minimal pair after the speaker.

live/leave	white/right
think/sink	side/sight
town/down	beach/peach
harbour/arbour	

C Discriminating between minimal pairs of sounds 1

Listen and underline which word you hear.

1. I think we should **leave/live** here.
2. I can see you're **sinking/thinking**.
3. I can see **he's down/his town**.
4. What a beautiful **arbour/harbour**!
5. Isn't that **right/white**?
6. Which **side/sight** are you talking about?
7. What a wonderful **beach/peach**!

D Contractions

Contractions are common in informal spoken and written English, such as two friends chatting, emails between friends, and so on, but not in more formal English such as lectures, speeches and letters to companies.

Look at the following excerpts from the interview and put in the contracted forms of the underlined words. Then listen to find out if you were correct.

Example: <u>I have</u> never been to Dover. **I've**

1. <u>It is</u> mainly just a harbour town. _____
2. there <u>are not</u> many to see _____
3. <u>that is</u> about it _____
4. it <u>was not</u> sand _____
5. but you <u>do not</u> know if <u>they are</u> still cave entrances
   _____/_____
6. unless <u>you have</u> got transport _____

E Sentence stress

Stressed words are the most important in spoken English because they carry the most meaning. Which words are stressed in the following extracts?

1. Now you used to live in Dover, I think?
2. It's mainly just a harbour town . . .
3. people go there to cross the Channel to France
4. you have the tour bus that goes round to see the sights of Dover
5. the castle's the main attraction
6. The view was nice.
7. But the beach was nothing special because it wasn't sand. It was stones.
8. There are parts of it that are nice.

F Recognising individual words in a stream of speech

Work with a partner. Listen to the excerpts from Danny's interview and write them down. Then check your answers with another pair.

1. _____
2. _____
3. _____
4. _____
5. _____

G Hearing the sounds of English 2

As with Exercise B, listen and repeat each minimal pair after the speaker.

right/light	been/bin
main/man	still/steel
bus/buzz	while/whirl
view/phew	

H Discriminating between minimal pairs of sounds 2

Tick (✓) the boxes which correspond to the words you hear.

1	1	2	3	4	5
right					
light					
2	1	2	3	4	5
main					
man					
3	1	2	3	4	5
bus					
buzz					
4	1	2	3	4	5
view					
phew					
5	1	2	3	4	5
been					
bin					
6	1	2	3	4	5
still					
steel					
7	1	2	3	4	5
while					
whirl					

I Weak forms

The pronunciation of *to*, *for* and *of* often changes to a weaker form in spoken English which is not as clear.

Try to fill in the missing words in these excerpts and then listen to check your answers. How does the pronunciation of *to*, *for* and *of* change in informal spoken English?

1. I've never been _____ Dover.
2. not a lot _____ people there
3. basically people go there _____ cross the Channel
4. The sea's surprisingly blue, _____ England.
5. Now they talk about the White Cliffs _____ Dover.
6. A lot _____ restaurants.
7. You have the tour bus that goes round _____ see the sights _____ Dover.
8. If you just go over _____ the day, Calais's about as far as you can go.

J Gap-fill – elision

When speaking quickly in English, people often miss out individual sounds at the ends of words — a process known as elision. For example, a speaker will say *las' night* instead of *last night*, *jus' got here* instead of *just got here*, or *trie' to* instead of *tried to*.

Try to fill in the missing words in these extracts, all of which have been affected by elision.

1. Now you _____ _____ live in Dover, I think.
2. You have the tour bus that _____ _____ to see the sights of Dover.
3. It _____ _____ you round the, round the beach area . . .
4. If you _____ _____ over for the day, Calais's about as far as you can go.

5. Further Language Development

A Extension exercise

Fill in the blanks with words you heard during Danny's interview.

> beach   companies   expensive   ferry   harbour
> population   sea   stones   student   used   view

1. I _____ to like sugar in my tea when I was young, but now I find it too sweet.

2. What is the _____ of London? Is it eight million?

3. The next _____ to Sweden leaves in half an hour.

4. There is a very nice sandy _____ in Bournemouth which is wonderful for young children to play on.

5. I have a wonderful _____ of the sea from my office window.

6. These restaurants are all very _____. Shall we go to a café instead?

7. My brother is a _____ at this college.

8. When the weather is very bad, most ships stay in the _____.

9. I've got interviews next week with two different _____ — one in Bristol and one in Birmingham.

10. I don't like swimming in the _____ in this country because it's too cold. I prefer a swimming pool.

11. These _____ hurt your feet, don't they? I wish I'd worn better shoes, but I didn't know we were going for a walk on the beach.

B Introduction to the present perfect simple

We use the present perfect simple to talk about things that have, or haven't happened during a period of time leading up the present. To form the present perfect simple we use the verb *to have + past participle.*

Put the verbs in brackets into the present perfect simple.

1. I (live) _____ here since 2005.

2. Peter (lose) _____ 10 kilos since he started that diet.

3. Sorry, I (use) _____ all the milk.

4. We (buy) _____ a new car!

5. I (finish) _____ my homework at last.

6. I (post) _____ your letter.

7. Phil and Sam (move) _____ to New York.

8. Oh no! Yuko (leave) _____ her mobile phone behind.

9. I (decide) _____ to get a new job.

10. Is it true you (stop) _____ eating meat?

C Prepositions

Put the correct prepositions in the gaps. Some of them are used more than once.

> about   for   in   of   on   to

1. I used to live _____ Chicago, but last year I moved _____ New York.

2. Tell me all _____ your holiday!

3. I can't come out tonight. I've got a lot _____ work to do.

4. My idea of a perfect holiday is lying _____ a beach with a good book.

5. It gets very cold here _____ the winter.

6. She's very grown-up _____ her age.

7. When we looked out of our window we saw the car was covered _____ snow.

8. Which part _____ Bulgaria do you come from?

9. We're going _____ Russia next month _____ a wedding.

10. Could you sit _____ the other side _____ Rachel?

D Transformations

Change the word in each bracket which Danny used in his interview to form a word which fits the gap.

1. What subject are you (student) _____ at university?

2. How much does it cost to go from Dover to Calais by (ferries) _____?

3. I've got a wonderful (surprisingly) _____ for your birthday!

4. Our hotel was right next to a beautiful (sand) _____ beach.

5. I don't like going to London in the summer because it's always full of (tour) _____.

I: OK. Now you used to live in Dover, I think?

D: I did (1) a placement in Dover in my third year.

I: In your third year 'cos, 'cos you're a student.

D: That's right.

I: Third year was in Dover. I've never been to Dover. Can you tell me a bit about the town?

D: It's mainly just (2) a harbour town, with . . .

I: Right. So lots of ships . . . coming in.

D: . . . what you'd expect from a harbour town. Very small, not a lot of people there, small (3) population, and, like you said, (4) basically people go there to cross (5) the Channel to France.

I: OK. So they have big (6) ferries there?

D: Big ferries, (7) hovercraft, two big main companies: Sea France and P&O Ferries.

I: Um, is the town nice?

D: No.

I: No. (laughs)

D: (8) It portrays that it is nice, 'cos you have (9) the tour bus that goes round to see (10) the sights of Dover, but there aren't many to see.

I: What are they, then?

D: Well, (11) the castle's the main attraction. (12) The cliffs, (13) obviously and um . . . that's about it. It just takes you round the, round the (14) beach area um, which is where my hotel was, on the beach area.

I: Oh, that must have been nice.

D: The (15) view was nice. (laughs)

I: Mmm, hmm.

D: But not in the winter.

I: Right, but, but . . . sort of like in the summer, was the sea blue and . . .?

D: The sea's (16) surprisingly blue, for England.

I: Mmm, hmm. Right.

D: But the beach was nothing special because it wasn't (17) sand. It was (18) stones.

I: Right.

D: So it wasn't too comfortable.

I: Mmm, hmm.

D: But it was a nice view.

I: Now they talk about the White Cliffs of Dover. Are they really white?

D: Very white. You must have seen pictures.

I: I've seen pictures, yeah. But I've, I've never been to Dover.

D: They are really white. Some are covered in (19) forestry, but mostly white.

I: What – trees and (20) bushes and . . .

D: Trees and bushes and you still have the odd, um, the odd . . . it's sort of . . . it's hard to explain. You see kind of (21) cave entrances halfway up the cliff, but you don't know if they're still cave entrances. I think they might be past, part of the castle, the und . . . underneath.

I: Sort of (22) tunnels.

D: Tunnels.

I: (23) To store things.

D: I've never been. I never did the tour.

I: OK.

D: (24) I never got a chance. It was quite expensive. But yeah, I think they're the tunnels of the castle.

I: Right. OK. Um, did you ever go to France while you were living in Dover?

D: I did. Didn't get any further than Calais.

I: Mmm.

D: But that's about all you can do is . . . unless you've got (25) transport, go over with transport. If you just go over for the day, Calais's about as far as you can go.

I: (26) But Calais's supposed to be a nice place.

D: There are parts of it that are nice. A lot of restaurants. Um, but it's mainly just a small French harbour town, like Dover is, on the other side of the water.

I: Has it got a beach there?

D: It does . . . with sand.

I: Oh, right.

D: (laughs) Which is (27) a bonus.

1. **a placement** – Business Studies students often spend part of their studies working for a company which may be some distance away from their university.
2. **a harbour town** – a town near an area of water next to the coast often protected from the sea by a thick wall, where ships and boats can dock
3. **population** – the number of people living in a country or place, e.g. What's the population of New York City?
4. **basically** – the most important thing is that . . .
5. **the Channel** – (the English Channel) the area of water separating England from France
6. **ferries** (plural) **a ferry**– A ferry is a boat used to transport passengers and vehicles across water as a regular service.
7. **(a) hovercraft** – a vehicle which goes over water or land on a cushion of air
8. **It portrays that it is nice** – (unusual usage) It gives the impression that it is nice.
9. **the tour bus** – a bus which takes people to the most interesting parts of the town
10. **the sights** (plural) – the places of interest, especially to visitors
11. **the castle's the main attraction** – the reason most people visit Dover is to see the castle – the large old stone building on top of the cliffs
12. **The cliffs** (plural) – A cliff is a high area of rock or chalk with very steep sides, often on the coast.
13. **obviously** – it's easy to understand why
14. **(a) beach** – an area of sand or small stones beside the sea
15. **(a) view** – what you can see from a particular place
16. **surprisingly blue** – unexpectedly blue, more blue than you would think
17. **sand** – very small grains of rock found on beaches or in deserts such as the Sahara
18. **stones** (plural) **a stone**– small pieces of rock
19. **forestry** – (unusual usage) The real meaning of forestry is planting and looking after trees. Danny means forests – a forest is a large area of land with trees.
20. **bushes** (plural) – A bush is a plant smaller than a tree with lots of small, thin branches.
21. **(a) cave** – a large hole in the side of a hill, cliff or mountain
22. **tunnels** (plural) **a tunnel**– A tunnel is a long passage through the earth, often made by people.
23. **To store things.** – To put or keep things in a special place for future use.
24. **I never got a chance.** – I never had the opportunity to do this.
25. **transport** – (in this case) if you have your own car or motorbike
26. **But Calais's supposed to be a nice place.** – But people say Calais is a nice place.
27. **a bonus** – (in this case) a pleasant extra thing

UNIT 2 Catherine

1. Pre-Listening Comprehension

Catherine grew up in the small market town of Llanrwst in North Wales and has lived there ever since. She is bilingual in Welsh and English and she has a strong North Welsh accent. Catherine is a pensioner but she still works as a bookkeeper. The nearest major town to Llanrwst is Llandudno.

A Welsh pronunciation

If a Welsh word begins with *ll*, as in the town *Llanrwst*, it is pronounced by placing the tongue loosely across the top of the mouth and breathing out through your cheeks.

However, people outside Wales usually ignore this and pronounce the double *l* as a single *l*. Try to say *Llanelli*.

In Welsh the letter *w* in a word is pronounced as the letter *u*, so Llanrwst is actually pronounced 'Llanroost'.

In Welsh the letter *u* is pronounced as the letter *i*, so Llandudno is actually pronounced 'Llandidno' by Welsh people.

The letter *y* in Welsh is pronounced as the letter *u*, so the word for Wales – Cymru – is actually pronounced 'Cumree'.

B Normalisation – anticipating the next word

 to

 to

Listen to tracks 26–30. There is a word missing from the end of each excerpt. Try to guess the missing word and write it down. Then listen to tracks 31–35 to check your answers. How well did you guess?

1. _____
2. _____
3. _____
4. _____
5. _____

2. Listening Comprehension

A Corrections

Catherine talks about the small town of Llanrwst. Correct the mistake in each sentence.

1. Llanrwst is a large market town.
2. The bridge was built by Inigo James.
3. He built the bridge in 1638.
4. Llanrwst has lots of visitors in winter.
5. The café in the cottage looks beautiful in the spring.
6. The cricket team play on Sundays.
7. There are mountains on one side of the valley and trees on the other.

B Gap-fill

Catherine talks about going down to the nearest major town, Llandudno.

Before you listen, try to predict which words, or which types of words (nouns, adjectives, prepositions, parts of verbs, etc.) will fit in the gaps. Then listen and check your answers.

1. Catherine can see _____ from the back of her house.
2. There are _____ each side of the road from Llanrwst to Llandudno.
3. The road follows the _____ down to the sea.
4. There are beautiful _____ along the promenade in Llandudno.
5. Catherine goes to Llandudno at least once a _____.

C Questions

Catherine talks about a typical day out in Llandudno. Listen and answer the questions.

1. Which supermarket does Catherine go to?
2. Who does she take with her?
3. What day do they usually go to Llandudno?
4. What is *The Cottage Loaf*?
5. What does Catherine's friend love buying?
6. What time does Catherine usually come home from her day in Llandudno?

D Corrections

Catherine talks about housework and a typical Saturday. Correct the mistake in each sentence.

1. Catherine's husband hates doing the washing.
2. Catherine does the ironing on Monday mornings.
3. On Saturdays she meets her friends for lunch.
4. They spend two hours together.

A The present simple

Catherine uses the present simple when she talks about things which happen regularly, as in the following examples:

> they _play_ cricket there
> Lots of people _go_ and _watch_ it on a Saturday afternoon.
> I _do_ my shopping in Asda there.
> We _do_ our shopping in Asda.
> we _meet_ in a little old-fashioned café . . .

B _Used to_ (do something) for past habit

As with Danny in Unit 1, Catherine uses _used to_ when she talks about the old tennis courts.

> There used to be tennis courts there . . .

Here are some more examples of this usage:

> 'There used to be a field here, but now it's a car park.'
> 'I'm sure there used to be a tree here.'
> 'This room used to be a bedroom but now I use it as my office.'

C The simple past

Catherine uses the simple past passive when she talks about the bridge over the River Conway in Llanrwst.

> and an old bridge which _was built_ by Inigo Jones in 1636

To form the simple past passive we use the simple past of the verb _to be_ and add the past participle. Here are some more examples:

> 'The Taj Mahal _was built_ between 1630 and 1653.'
> 'The Lord of the Rings movies _were filmed_ in New Zealand.'
> 'This photo of me _was taken_ in 1997.'

D *It is* and *There are*

When we are talking about something for the first time we generally say *There is . . .*, whereas when we are giving details about something we have already referred to we say *It is . . ..*

Look at these examples from the interview where Catherine mentions things in Llanrwst for the first time:

> <u>There's</u> a river flowing through it . . .
> And <u>there's</u> a putting place on the um, the other side of the river.
> <u>There's</u> a nice bowling green there.

Now look at these examples where Catherine is giving details about Llanrwst:

> Well, <u>it's</u> a little market town. It's a pretty little town.
> Yes, <u>it's</u> a very pleasant place to live.

Later she talks about her husband doing the washing. She says:

> And <u>it's</u> usually dry and folded by the time I get home.

---

4. Further Listening Practice

A Sentence stress

 to

Speakers stress the words they feel are important to convey their meaning. Which words are stressed in the following extracts?

1. It's a pretty little town.
2. it has lots of visitors in summer
3. beautiful colour in the autumn
4. There's a nice bowling green there.
5. Yes, it's a very pleasant place to live.
6. we have a day out on a Friday, usually
7. We do our shopping in Asda.

B Hearing the sounds of English 1

Listen and repeat each minimal pair after the speaker.

river/liver   clothes/crows
watch/wash   washing/watching
back/pack   dry/try
shopping/chopping

C Discriminating between minimal pairs of sounds 1

Listen and underline which word you hear.

1. This **river/liver** is wonderful!
2. You need a **watch/wash**.
3. My **back/pack** is hurting.
4. You do the **shopping/chopping** and I'll do the cooking.
5. What a lot of **clothes/crows**!
6. He's always **washing/watching** his car.
7. You must **dry/try** this.

D Weak forms

As with Danny's interview, the pronunciation of *to, for, from* and *of* has changed to a weaker form which is not as clear. Try to fill in the missing words in these excerpts and then listen to check your answers.

How has the pronunciation of *to, for, from* and *of* changed?

1. What kind _____ place is it?
2. So can you see mountains _____ your house?
3. So Llandudno is next _____ the sea, then . . .
4. Lots _____ people go and watch it on a Saturday afternoon.
5. What time do you come home _____ a day in Llandudno?
6. Then I go out and meet a couple of my friends _____ coffee.

E Hearing the sounds of English 2

As with Exercise B, listen and repeat each minimal pair after the speaker.

town/down	very/ferry
old/hold	next/nest
green/grin	called/cold
back/pack	

F Discriminating between minimal pairs of sounds 2

Tick (✓) the boxes which correspond to the words you hear.

1	1	2	3	4	5
town					
down					

2	1	2	3	4	5
old					
hold					

3	1	2	3	4	5
green					
grin					

4	1	2	3	4	5
back					
pack					

5	1	2	3	4	5
very					
ferry					

6	1	2	3	4	5
next					
nest					

7	1	2	3	4	5
called					
cold					

G 'um' for pauses

When people are talking they often say 'um' while they are giving themselves time to think about what they are going to say next. What sounds do you make in your own language when you are pausing?

Listen and mark where Catherine uses 'um' in the following excerpts:

1. And it has lots of visitors in summer.

2. And there's a putting place on the the other side of the river.

3. and they play cricket there . . .

4. we meet in a little old-fashioned café called the Hên Aelwyd . . . only 11 till 12.

H Recognising individual words in a stream of speech – dictation

 to

Work with a partner. Listen to the excerpts from Catherine's interview and write them down. Then check your answers with another pair.

1. _____ .

2. _____ .

3. _____ . . .

4. _____ .

5. _____ ?

6. _____ ?

7. _____ ?

8. _____ .

9. _____ .

I Hearing the sounds of English 3

As with Exercises B and E, listen and repeat each minimal pair after the speaker.

built/build	meet/mitt
team/Tim	side/sight
live/leave	quite/quiet
first/thirst	

J Discriminating between minimal pairs of sounds 3

Tick (✓) the boxes which correspond to the words you hear.

1	1	2	3	4	5
built					
build					
2	1	2	3	4	5
team					
Tim					
3	1	2	3	4	5
live					
leave					
4	1	2	3	4	5
first					
thirst					
5	1	2	3	4	5
meet					
mitt					
6	1	2	3	4	5
side					
sight					
7	1	2	3	4	5
quite					
quiet					

K Linking

As with Danny's interview there are numerous examples of linking in this interview.

Linking occurs when the end of one word runs_into the start_of the next word. It is very common in informal spoken English, but less so in more formal English, such as speeches or lectures.

The most common linking occurs between the letter *-s* at the end of a word when the next word begins with a vowel, as in these excerpts from the interview. However, linking also occurs with other sounds.

Mark where linking occurs in these excerpts from the interview.

1. Well, it's a little market town.

2. It's a pretty little town.

3. There's a river owing through it . . .

4. it has lots of visitors in summer

5. There's a nice bowling green there.

6. Round the back of it, yes, easily.

7. 'Queen of Resorts of North Wales', they reckon.

8. Beautiful hotels along the promenade . . .

9. Once a week at least, yes.

10. And it's usually dry and folded by the time I get home.

L Gap-fill – elision

As we heard in Danny's interview, when speaking quickly in English, people often miss out individual sounds at the ends of words — a process known as elision. For example, a speaker will say *las' night* instead of *last night*, *jus' got here* instead of *just got here*, or *trie' to* instead of *tried to*.

Fill in the missing words in these extracts, all of which have been affected by elision.

1. Well, it's a little _____ _____.

2. and an _____ _____

3. There _____ _____ be tennis courts there . . .

4. _____ the back of it, yes, easily

5. Yes, it's a very _____ place to live.

6. So Llandudno is _____ _____ the sea, then . . .

7. _____ my friend

8. We'll have gone _____ _____ in the morning.

A Extension exercise

Fill in the blanks with words you heard during Catherine's interview.

> been   colour   cottage   dry   field   hotels
> husband   living   mountains   river   sea
> shopping   tennis   tiny   town   watch

1. A place which is bigger than a village, but smaller than a city is called a _____.

2. The best place to go fishing in this _____ is near the old bridge.

3. My sister lives in a tiny old _____ in the country.

4. What _____ is your new car?

5. In the summer I play _____ and in the winter I play squash.

6. Lots of people _____ television before they go to work.

7. The highest _____ in Norway always have snow on them, even in summer.

8. There is a big _____ behind my friend's house which is full of sheep.

9. The River Conway ows into the _____ at Llandudno.

10. They say _____ in New York are very expensive. Even a cheap one costs at least $100 a night.

11. Your feet are _____! Mine are twice as big as yours!

12. My _____ and I share the housework.

13. This plant is very _____. Shall I give it some water?

14. I've never _____ to Turkey.

15. We always go _____ on Thursdays.

16. How long have you been _____ in this at?

B Gap–fill

This is a revision exercise. You will probably be able to complete it correctly, even without hearing the extract again. The missing words are listed in the box. One of the words is used twice.

Try to predict the missing words before you listen. Then listen and check your answers.

> called   first   friends   home   husband   loves
> lunch   our   out   past   street   time   washing

Catherine: We do **(1)** _____ shopping in Asda. Park there. Go up town. Park there again. Have **(2)** _____ in a little . . . little tiny pub **(3)** _____ the Cottage Loaf. And then we do the shopping at the main **(4)** _____, for my friend **(5)** _____ to shop for clothes and things. (*laughs*)

Interviewer: What time do you come **(6)** _____ from a day in Llandudno?

Catherine: Oh, about **(7)** half-_____ four. We'll have gone about 10 in the morning. And my poor **(8)** _____ is home doing the **(9)** _____, every week, which he **(10)** _____. And it's usually dry and folded by the **(11)** _____ I get home.

Interviewer: Does your husband do the ironing as well?

Catherine: No, no, no. I do that **(12)** _____ thing on a Saturday morning. Then I go **(13)** _____ and meet a couple of my **(14)** _____ for coffee.

C The present simple and present continuous

We generally use the present simple to talk about things that happen regularly, as in this example from Catherine's interview:

> We _do_ our shopping in Asda.

We generally use the present continuous to talk about things we are doing at the moment, as in this example:

> 'It's my birthday and I _am having_ a wonderful day.'

Put the verbs in brackets into either the present simple or the present continuous, as appropriate.

1. Can you speak a bit louder? Adrian (cut) _____ the grass and I can't hear you very well.
2. Normally I (do) _____ all the cooking at the weekend.
3. My sister (study) _____ to be a lawyer.
4. We (go) _____ to Canada at least twice a year.
5. I usually (start) _____ work at 9, but sometimes I (go) _____ in earlier.
6. Sarah (play) _____ in the garden. Shall I get her for you?
7. This train (go) _____ really slowly. I'm sure we're going to be late.

D Transformations

Change the word in each bracket which Catherine used in her interview to form a word which fits the gap.

1. This is the (pretty) _____ village I've ever seen.
2. Who is the (old) _____ of your brothers and sisters?
3. This (built) _____ wasn't here when I was a girl.
4. Don't forget to (covered) _____ the fish with milk before cooking.
5. I drew the picture and then Daisy (colour) _____ it in. Isn't it great?
6. Who's your favourite football (play) _____?
7. I'm (watch) _____ a really interesting programme. Can I call you back?
8. I think you'll find it's (easily) _____ to open if you take the plastic off.
9. The best (shopping) _____ are at the other end of High Street.
10. I like her new boyfriend. He's much (friend) _____ than her last one.
11. Can you seek a (park) _____ space anywhere?

I: Can you um, tell me about Llanrwst? What kind of place is it?

C: Well, it's a little **(1) market town**. It's a pretty little town. There's a river owing through it – the River Conway – and an old **(2) bridge** which was built by Inigo Jones in 1636 I think. And um, it has lots of visitors in summer. The other side of this bridge is a very old **(3) cottage** that er, is very pretty. **(4) It's covered with ivy** and . . . beautiful colour in the autumn.

I: Mmm, hmm.

C: And they sell **(5) cream teas** and so the coaches come and have their **(6) scone**, **(7) jam** and **(8) cream**. And there's **(9) a putting place** on the um, the other side of the river. There used to be tennis courts there but they've done away with those. There's a nice **(10) bowling green** there. They have quite a good **(11) team** in Llanrwst. Um, and they play cricket there and they have a good cricket team as well. Lots of people go and watch it on a Saturday afternoon.

I: And is it in **(12) a valley** or up **(13) a mountain**?

C: Yes. Beautiful valley, the Conway Valley – mountains one side, quite high mountains – and **(14) fields** the other.

I: So can you see mountains from your house?

C: Oh yes, yes. Round the back of it, yes, easily. Yes, it's a very **(15) pleasant** place to live. And all the way down to the largest town which is Llandudno, **(16) a beautiful run with trees** and . . . all the way down, each side of the road.

I: And does the road follow the river down?

C: Yes, all the way down . . . to the sea, of course.

I: So Llandudno is next to the sea, then . . . or on the sea.

C: Yes. Qu . . . **(17) 'Queen of Resorts of North Wales'**, **(18) they reckon**. It is, too. It's very pretty. **(19) It hasn't been altered, hardly.** Beautiful hotels along **(20) the promenade**, and um . . .

I: Do you go there quite often?

C: Oh yes. Once a week at least, yes. Actually I do my shopping in **(21) Asda** there.

I: Oh right.

C: Take my friend and er, we have a day out on a Friday, usually.

I: So you have lunch out and . . .

C: We have. We do our shopping in Asda. **(22) Park there.** Go up town. Park there again. Have lunch in a little. . . little **(23) tiny** **(24) pub** called **(25) the Cottage Loaf**. And then we do the shopping at the main street, for my friend loves to shop for clothes and things. (*laughs*)

I: What time do you come home from a day in Llandudno?

C: Oh, about half-past four. We'll have gone about 10 in the morning. And my poor husband is home **(26) doing the washing**, every week, which he loves. And **(27) it's usually dry and folded** by the time I get home.

I: Does your husband do **(28) the ironing** as well?

C: No, no, no. I do that first thing on a Saturday morning. Then I go out and meet **(29) a couple of my friends** for coffee.

I: Do you go to their houses?

C: No, we meet in a little old-fashioned **(30) café** called **(31) the Hên Aelwyd**. . . . Um, only 11 till 12. Home, then, for lunch. And then whatever Saturday afternoon . . .

1. **(a) market town** – a small town in the country which is a business centre for farms and villages in the area
2. **(a) bridge** – something built over a river to allow people, vehicles or trains to cross from one side to the other
3. **(a) cottage** – a small house usually in the countryside
4. **It's covered with ivy** – Ivy is an evergreen plant which often grows up trees and buildings. Catherine has made a mistake here: in fact the plant which covers the cottage is Virginia creeper which changes from green in the summer to red in the autumn.
5. **cream teas** (plural) – A cream tea is a light meal in the afternoon where you have a pot of tea, scones, jam and cream.
6. **(a) scone** – a small, round type of cake
7. **jam** – a very thick sweet food made from boiled fruit and sugar and often eaten on toast
8. **cream** – the thick liquid which forms on the top of milk
9. **a putting place** – a small   at area of short grass where people can practise hitting golf balls into holes
10. **(a) bowling green** – a   at area of short grass where people play the game of bowls
11. **(a) team** – a group of people who do something together, for example a football team, a cricket team
12. **a valley** – an area of low land between hills or mountains often with a river running through it
13. **a mountain** – something much larger than a hill
14. **fields** (plural) – A field is a large area of land in the country where farmers grow things or where a farmer's animals feed on grass.
15. **pleasant** – nice
16. **a beautiful run** – a beautiful drive in the car
17. **'Queen of Resorts of North Wales'** – Another way of saying the best resort in North Wales. A resort is a place where people go on holiday.
18. **they reckon** – they say; this is their opinion
19. **It hasn't been altered, hardly.** – It hasn't changed very much over the years.
20. **the promenade** – a wide road next to the sea which people can walk or drive along
21. **Asda** – one of the UK's largest supermarket chains
22. **Park there.** – (We) leave the car there.
23. **tiny** – very, very small
24. **(a) pub** – a building where people go to drink alcoholic and non-alcoholic drinks, to eat and to meet friends
25. **the Cottage Loaf** – A cottage loaf is a loaf of bread which has a small round part on top of a larger round part. In this case it is the name of the pub.
26. **doing the washing** – putting the dirty clothes in the washing machine and then drying them
27. **it's usually dry and folded** – Dry is the opposite of wet. Folded means to bend the clothes so that they lie on top of each other in a pile.
28. **the ironing** – using a hot iron to make clothes   at and smooth
29. **a couple of my friends** – two or three of my friends
30. **(a) café** – a small kind of restaurant where you can buy non-alcoholic drinks and simple meals
31. **the Hên Aelwyd** – 'Hên' is a Welsh word meaning 'old' and 'Aelwyd' is a Welsh word which means the hearth or fireplace in a home where the family would sit in front of the fire and talk.

UNIT 3 Anders

1. Pre-Listening Comprehension

A Discussion

Anders lives and works in Gothenburg in Sweden. He originally qualified as an English and German teacher, but he now works for one of Sweden's biggest training companies. He and his partner live in a new flat near a canal. Anders speaks very good English with a slight Swedish accent.

1. What do you think of when you hear the word 'Sweden'?
2. How much do you know about Sweden?

B Normalisation – gap-fill

This exercise is designed to help you get used to Anders's voice. Try to guess the missing words before you listen and discuss these with your teacher. Then listen and fill in the gaps.

1. Anders came to Gothenburg to study at the _____.
2. After his studies he got a _____ in Gothenburg.
3. He lives close to the _____.
4. Gothenburg used to be famous for _____-building.
5. Sweden experienced a financial crisis in _____.
6. The area where Anders lives was _____ for a long time.

2. Listening Comprehension

A Questions

Anders talks about the area where he lives. Listen and answer the questions.

1. Does Anders live in a house or a at?
2. Where does he take the ferry to?
3. How long does the ferry journey from Anders's home to central Gothenburg take?
4. How long is it on foot from Anders's home to the ferry stop?

B True/false

Anders talks some more about living in Gothenburg. Answer true or false. Be prepared to give reasons for your answers.

1. _____ Anders has a fantastic view of the water from his house.
2. _____ Anders lives less than a minute from the waterfront.
3. _____ It's possible to take a ferry from central Gothenburg to Denmark and Norway.
4. _____ Anders often sees these big ferries.

C Corrections

Anders talks about Åmål, the town where he grew up. Correct the mistake in each of these sentences.

1. Åmål is about 200 miles north of Gothenburg.
2. It has around 50,000 inhabitants.
3. Anders said it was possible to cycle anywhere in Åmål.
4. There was a big fire in Åmål in the 1800s.
5. There are still lots of wooden houses in Åmål from the old days.
6. Lake Vänern is the biggest lake in Sweden.

D Gap-fill

Anders talks about his mother. Before you listen, try to predict which words, or which types of words (nouns, adjectives, prepositions, parts of verbs, etc.) will fit in the gaps. Then listen and check your answers.

1. Anders goes to _____ his mother in Åmål regularly.
2. He goes to see her in Åmål more _____ than she comes to visit him in Gothenburg.
3. This is because she's quite elderly and she finds it difficult to walk and to sit in a _____ or get on a _____.
4. Anders and his mother often speak to each other on the _____.

A The present simple

1. The present simple (permanent situations)

We generally use the present simple when we are talking about situations which we see as permanent. Look at these examples from the interview:

> *Per-Olov said you <u>come</u> from his home town . . .*
> *I <u>live</u> very near to the . . . very near the water.*
> *the biggest ones [ships] <u>don't go</u> into town*
> *she <u>finds</u> it difficult to walk*

To form a question in the present simple we use ***do/does + verb***:

> *And <u>do</u> you <u>live</u> in Gothenburg now?*

2. The present simple (routines and regular actions)

We also use the present simple when we are talking about routines and things that happen regularly.

> *I <u>see</u> them [the ferries] more or less every day.*
> *I <u>go</u> up to visit her more often than she <u>comes</u> down to Gothenburg*
> *We <u>talk</u> on the phone very, very often, though.*

And again we use ***do/does + verb*** to form questions:

> *<u>Do</u> you ever <u>go</u> back to Åmål?*
> *And <u>does</u> she ever <u>come</u> down to Gothenburg?*

B The simple past

1. The simple past (regular verbs)

We use the simple past to talk about completed actions in the past, usually with reference to a time in the past. To form the simple past of regular verbs we simply add **–ed**.

The first example is when Anders talks about what happened to the land where his flat was built. After the financial crisis of 1976 it was empty for years, and then:

> *all of a sudden they <u>started</u> building er, flats*

The second example comes when Anders talks about growing up in Åmål. He says:

you <u>had</u> everything you <u>needed</u>

2. The simple past (verbs ending in –*e*)

If a verb already ends in –*e*, we simply add –*d* to form the simple past:

I <u>moved</u> away from there when I was in my 20s . . .
they <u>used</u> to build ships in Gothenburg.

3. The simple past (irregular verbs)

There are several irregular verbs in the interview and it is a good idea to learn these. Remember, if you don't know the past tense of a verb you can just add –*ed*. Any native speaker, or competent non-native speaker, will understand your meaning.

Per-Olov <u>said</u> you come from his home town . . .
can you tell me about where you <u>grew</u> up
it <u>burnt</u> down in the 1600s

C The present perfect simple with *for* and *since*

We use the present perfect simple to talk about things which have (or haven't) happened during a period of time leading up to the present. To form the present perfect simple we use the *verb have + past participle*. We often use the present perfect simple with *for* and *since*. Look at these examples:

1. The present perfect simple with *for*:

'I <u>have lived</u> here <u>for</u> nine years.'
'He <u>hasn't seen</u> her <u>for</u> weeks.'
'He <u>hasn't had</u> anything to eat <u>for</u> hours.'
'We <u>have had</u> no rain <u>for</u> days.'

2. The present perfect simple with *since*:

'I <u>have lived</u> here <u>since</u> 2001.'
'I <u>have been</u> here <u>since</u> 2 o'clock.'

'He <u>hasn't eaten</u> anything <u>since</u> breakfast.'

'We <u>have had</u> brilliant weather <u>since</u> May.'

Now look at this example of the present perfect simple with *since* taken from the interview:

I live in Gothenburg now and I've lived there ever since I started university ...

A **Recognising individual words in a stream of speech – dictation**

  to

Work with a partner. Listen to the excerpts from Anders's interview and write them down. Then check your answers with another pair.

1. _____.

2. _____

3. _____?

4. _____.

5. _____.

6. _____.

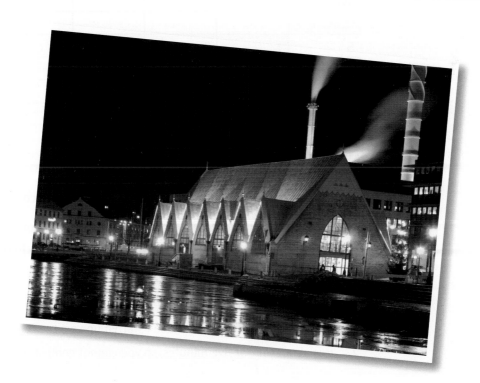

B Hearing the sounds of English 1

Listen and repeat each minimal pair after the speaker.

his/is	live/leave
right/light	had/hat
think/sink	

C Discriminating between minimal pairs of sounds 1

Tick (✓) the boxes which correspond to the words you hear.

1	1	2	3	4	5
his					
is					
2	1	2	3	4	5
right					
light					
3	1	2	3	4	5
think					
sink					
4	1	2	3	4	5
live					
leave					
5	1	2	3	4	5
had					
hat					

D Contractions

Contractions are common in informal spoken and written English, such as two friends chatting, emails between friends, and so on, but not in more formal English such as lectures, speeches and letters to companies.

Look at the following excerpts from the interview and put in the contracted forms of the underlined words. Then listen to find out if you were correct.

Example: Yes, <u>that is</u> right. **that's**

1. and <u>I have lived</u> there ever since I started university . . . _____

2. <u>It is</u> about four or five minutes, so you <u>cannot</u> complain.
   _____ / _____

3. <u>That is</u> quite nice. _____

4. the biggest ones <u>do not</u> go into town _____

5. <u>they are</u> too big _____

6. So you said <u>it is</u> 200 kilometres north of Gothenburg. _____

7. Yeah. <u>That is</u> the second-biggest er, lake in Sweden. _____

8. <u>That is</u> a bit confusing. _____

9. <u>I have</u> still got my mother up there . . . _____

10. <u>she is</u> quite old. _____

E Hearing the sounds of English 2

As with Exercise B, listen and repeat each minimal pair after the speaker.

years/jeers	back/pack
north/Norse	grew/glue
old/hold	

F Discriminating between minimal pairs of sounds 2

Tick (✓) the boxes which correspond to the words you hear.

1	1	2	3	4	5
years					
jeers					
2	1	2	3	4	5
north					
Norse					
3	1	2	3	4	5
old					
hold					
4	1	2	3	4	5
back					
pack					
5	1	2	3	4	5
grew					
glue					

G Simplification – weak forms

As we heard with both Danny and Catherine, when we speak quickly a process known as 'simplification' occurs. Basically the speaker takes short cuts and doesn't articulate unstressed words fully. The term 'weak forms' refers to very common grammatical words such as prepositions whose pronunciation changes significantly in fast, informal spoken English. Some of the most common weak forms are *of, for, from* and *to.*

First predict which words fit in the gaps, then listen to check your answers.

1. the western part _____ Sweden

2. but I moved away _____ there when I was in my 20s

3. I moved _____ Gothenburg.

4. the area was empty _____ years and years

5. and then all _____ a sudden they started building er,   ats

6. you can actually take the ferry _____ work

7. nothing _____ that kind

How does the pronunciation of *to, for, from* and *of* change in informal spoken English?

H Hearing the sounds of English 3

As with Exercises B and E, listen and repeat each minimal pair after the speaker.

lake/rake	said/set
still/steel	all/hall
but/putt	

I **Discriminating between minimal pairs of sounds 3**

Tick (✓) the boxes which correspond to the words you hear.

1	1	2	3	4	5
lake					
rake					
2	1	2	3	4	5
still					
steel					
3	1	2	3	4	5
but					
putt					
4	1	2	3	4	5
said					
set					
5	1	2	3	4	5
all					
hall					

J **Simplification – elision**

As we heard with Danny and Catherine, when we speak quickly a process known as elision occurs – this is the missing out of sounds, particularly *-d* and *-t*. Elision makes it difficult for you to recognise even those words that are part of your active vocabulary.

Fill in the missing words in the following extracts from the interview, all of which have been affected by elision.

1. when I _____ _____ start my studies
2. I _____ _____ Gothenburg . . .
3. I've _____ _____ ever since I started university . . .
4. it's _____ _____ minutes
5. you _____ _____
6. the biggest ones _____ _____ into town
7. Yeah. That's the _____-_____ er, lake in Sweden.
8. That's a _____ _____ .
9. Do you ever go _____ _____ Åmål?

A Extension exercise

Fill in the blanks in these new sentences with words you heard during Anders's interview.

> build   burnt   complain   confusing
> empty   ferry   home   lake   left   moved
> since   toes   too   used   water

1. I'm going _____ — I'm really tired.

2. That park over there is where I _____ to play football when I was a kid.

3. We _____ here two years ago because we wanted a home with a garden.

4. I'm starving! I haven't had anything to eat _____ breakfast.

5. I love swimming, but I hate going under the _____.

6. The Government is going to _____ another 100,000 homes for the needy over the next five years.

7. I need to get some more petrol — the tank's nearly _____.

8. We started off in Athens and then we took a _____ to a nearby island.

9. I know it rained yesterday, but the weather's been wonderful for the past month or so, so we can't _____.

10. The instructor began the lesson by telling us to bend over and touch our _____.

11. We had the picnic under a tree because it was _____ hot to sit in the sun.

12. I'm sorry — I've _____ the toast again.

13. Is there any mashed potato _____? I'm really hungry.

14. At the top of the mountain there's a _____ where you can go swimming or sailing in summer.

15. The road signs were a bit _____ so I got lost twice, but I was only 20 minutes late.

B Verbs in the simple past

Change the verb stem in each bracket into the simple past. All the verbs are taken from the interview and appeared in the simple past.

1. We (move) _____ here in 2005.

2. When I was young I (want) _____ to be a train driver when I (grow) _____ up.

3. I (stop) _____ eating meat when I (be) _____ 17.

4. I (have) _____ to stay late at work yesterday because I (need) _____ to finish a report.

5. When I (be) _____ young I (can) _____ cycle up this hill without stopping!

6. Where's Peter got to? He (say) _____ he would be here at eight.

C Prepositions and adverbs

Put the correct preposition or adverb in the gaps. They are all taken from the interview. Some of them are used more than once.

> about   at   away   back   down   far   for   from
> in   into   near   of   on   since   to   up   with

1. Where do you come _____?

2. We live _____ north-east London.

3. I haven't seen you _____ ages.

4. Would you like some milk _____ your tea?

5. Can you get your dog _____ from the food, please?

6. I've been waiting for a bus _____ six o'clock.

7. Come round to my place tonight and tell me all _____ your holiday.

8. It's a beautiful house, but it's very _____ a main road, so there's always a lot _____ traffic noise, even _____ night.

9. How _____ is it from your house _____ the town centre?

10. I was walking along the street on my way to work when suddenly I walked _____ a lamp-post.

11. I can see Notre Dame Cathedral _____ my office window!

12. Someone stood _____ my toe on the subway and now it's black and blue.

13. I walked _____ and _____ the market for hours yesterday looking for strawberries.

14. Brighton is about 60 miles south _____ London _____ the south coast.

15. This garden reminds me _____ the one my grandmother had when I was growing _____.

16. I need to go _____ home. I think I left the window open.

17. My son's always _____ his mobile phone these days.

I: OK. Now um, Per-Olov said you come from his home town, which is Åmål, I think?

A: Yes, that's right. Er, I used to live there for 20 years and er, Åmål, that's a small little town er, in the western part of Sweden, with some 15 . . . 10 to 15,000 **(1) inhabitants**. Er, but I moved away from there when I was in my 20s when I had to . . . or when I wanted to start my studies, so I, I've . . . I moved to Gothenburg.

I: Right. And do you live in Gothenburg now?

A: I live in Gothenburg now and I've lived there ever since I started university and I got a job.

I: Right. OK. Um, so tell me about where you live in Gothenburg.

A: Er, I live very near to the . . . very near the water. Er, there have . . . they, they, they used to build ships in Gothenburg. It was very big until 1976 when everything was sort of stopped during **(2) the crisis** we had back then. And er, the area was empty for years and years and then **(3) all of a sudden** they started building er,   ats, and er, luckily enough I, I live in one of those over there, so the area is new, er, the   at is new and er, you can actually take **(4) the ferry** to work.

I: Really?

A: Which is quite nice!

I: (*laughs*) How far is it to get the ferry from where you live?

A: Er, it's about 20 minutes . . .

I: OK.

A: . . . from where I live into the central parts of Gothenburg.

I: OK. And do you have to walk long to **(5) the ferry stop**?

A: Er, not very long. It's about four or five minutes, so you can't complain.

I: Do you get . . . well, can you see the water from where you live?

A: Er, well, if I stand on my **(6) toes** I can . . .

I: Right.

A: . . . but er, it only takes . . . well, 30 seconds to reach the, the waterfront and um, that's quite nice.

I: Mmm. OK. Um, do you get ships going up and down **(7) the canal**?

A: Oh yes, er, the biggest ones don't go into town because . . . well, they're, they're too big, but er, we have the, the ferries going to Denmark and Germany and er, they go right into the centre of town, so I see them more or less every day.

I: Really?

A: That's quite nice.

I: Ah, brilliant.

I: OK. Um, can you tell me about where you grew up, which was Åmål, I think.

A: Yes, Åmål, that is about 200 kilometres north of Gothenburg. Er, **(8) a small, industrial town** with . . . well, 10 to 15,000 inhabitants. Er, it was really a **(9) calm**, nice, little . . . little town with er, well, all your friends, all your families – everybody was there and er, you had everything you needed and everything was er . . . I mean, you could walk anywhere.

I: Right.

A: No buses, no . . . nothing of that kind.

I: You said it was industrial. Was it a pretty town, or?

A: It is a really, really pretty town. Er, it was a wooden town but it burnt down in the 1600s and er, they had to rebuild all of it. So there are a, a few houses still left **(10) that reminds you of what it used to be like**, but er . . . yes, it's a, it's a really, really pretty town.

I: So you said it's 200 kilometres north of Gothenburg. Is it by the sea?

A: Er, yes. It's by er, the Väner, Väner Lake.

I: Oh, **(11) a lake**.

A: Yeah. That's the second-biggest er, lake in Sweden.

I: Mhm, hmm. So when you say 'sea', that . . . does that mean 'lake'?

A: That's means ja, it's a, it's a . . . ja, it means lake.

I: **(12) That's a bit confusing.**

A: It is. It certainly is.

I: Hmm. Do you ever go back to Åmål?

A: Yes. I've still got my mother up there, so I visit her regularly. Not as often as she wants, though, but er . . . I, I try to as often as I can.

I: Right. And does she ever come down to Gothenburg?

A: It happens, so . . . well, I go, I go up to visit her more often than she comes down to Gothenburg because er, she's quite old and she finds it difficult to walk and er, to sit in a car or to get onto a train or something. But er . . . we see each other. We talk on the phone very, very often, though.

I: OK. That's nice.

1 inhabitants (plural) an inhabitant– An inhabitant is someone who lives in a particular place.
2 the crisis – a time of suffering or uncertainty (in this case a financial crisis)
3 all of a sudden – very quickly
4 the ferry – a boat or ship taking passengers to and from places as a regular service
5 the ferry stop – the place where passengers get on or off a ferry
6 toes (plural) a toe – A toe is one of the the five separate points at the end of your feet (equivalent to the fingers on your hand).
7 the canal – a man-made channel for water
8 a small, industrial town – a small town where products are made in factories
9 calm – quiet, peaceful
10 that reminds you of what it used to be like – that gives you an idea of how it used to be
11 a lake – a large area of water surrounded by land
12 That's a bit confusing. – That's a little bit difficult to understand.

UNIT **4** Jackie

Normalisation

Jackie comes from Cardiff in South Wales, but she now lives in Cornwall in south-west England. Her accent is a mix of South Welsh and Cornish.

This exercise is designed to help you get used to Jackie's voice. Listen to the interview and write down as many words as you can.

Gap-fill

Jackie talks about her local area in Cornwall, in south-west England. Before you listen, try to predict which words, or which types of words (nouns, adjectives, prepositions, parts of verbs, etc.) will fit in the gaps. Then listen and check your answers.

1. Carlyon Bay is right on the _____.

2. Jackie and her husband live up the _____ from a small _____.

3. There is a beautiful _____ below them.

4. It's called _____ Harbour.

5. They keep '_____ ships' down in the harbour.

6. These are very old ships which they use when they make _____.

7. They filmed 'Mansfield _____' near where Jackie lives, and the last _____ Musketeers film.

8. Near the harbour there is also a _____.

9. There are beautiful _____ beaches all around Carlyon Bay.

10. Jackie says the whole area is wonderful, but very _____.

11. A lot of people come to Cornwall on _____.

A Extension exercise

Fill in the blanks in these new sentences with words you heard during Jackie's interview.

> beaches   been   fields   harbour   last
> like   make   tell   village   well   world

1. I've never _____ to Sweden. What's it _____?

2. Come and _____ me what you did at school today.

3. I grew up in a little _____ in the country, but I moved to London when I was 20.

4. The place we were staying in was right next to a _____ full of little fishing boats.

5. I think they should _____ a film about your life. You've done so many interesting things.

6. I prefer sandy _____ to ones with stones.

7. There are lots of sheep in the _____ behind our house.

8. My favourite city in the _____ is Munich.

9. That's the _____ time I lend you any money!

10. Shall we invite Anders as _____?

B Prepositions and adverbs

Put the correct preposition or adverb in the gaps. They are all taken from the interview. One of them is used twice.

> around   down   for   from   in
> like   of   on   over   to

1. Which US state is Boston _____? Is it Massachusetts?
2. We're going on holiday _____ Switzerland next week.
3. We've got a little holiday cottage _____ the west coast of Scotland.
4. This is the best knife _____ peeling potatoes.
5. When I have a day off I love walking _____ the shops.
6. We're just been _____ that new Mexican restaurant. It was brilliant!
7. What's your new manager _____? Do you get on with her?
8. We live about five minutes _____ the train station, so we can pick you up if you like.
9. My best friend lives _____ the road, so we see a lot _____ each other.
10. My cousin has travelled all _____ the world.

I: You live in (1) **Carlyon Bay**, I think, in (2) **Cornwall**.

J: Yes.

I: I've, I've never been to that (3) **area**. Can you tell me what it's like? Can you describe it to me?

J: It's right on the coast. Um . . .

I: Where, where you live is right on the coast?

J: Where, where I live, yes. (4) **We actually um, live up the fields from a small village on the coast.** There's a beautiful harbour down there. And er . . .

I: What's that called?

J: It's Charlestown Harbour. And er, they actually keep er,

(5) **tall ships** down there. There . . . these very old masted ships that they use er, they, they use them all over the world for, for making . . . in . . . when they make films. And er, they were used . . . last time they filmed down here they've, they've done (6) **Mansfield Park** and er, the last (7) **Three Musketeers** film was, was made down here. They do a lot of filming around Cornwall. And there's a nice . . . there's a harbour and a beach, and we have other beaches as well, beautiful sandy beaches. And we have (8) **the Eden Project**. And the, the whole area is, is wonderful. It's, it's er, very touristy, a lot of, lot of people come on holiday down here.

5. Words and Phrases

1 **Carlyon Bay** – The name of the bay is Carlyon. A bay is part of the coast where the land curves in a semi-circle.

2 **Cornwall** – the most south-westerly county in England

3 **(an) area** – a particular part of the country

4 **We actually um, live up the fields from a small village on the coast.** – Jackie is being more exact here. She doesn't really live right next to the sea, but she does live very close to it. The village is on the coast, then there are some fields and then there's Jackie's house.

5 **tall ships** – old ships with huge masts (A mast is the tall pole on a ship which supports the sails.)

6 **Mansfield Park** – a film based on the famous book of that title by Jane Austen

7 **(The) Three Musketeers** – three characters created by Alexandre Dumas in his books

8 **the Eden Project** – A popular tourist attraction in Cornwall consisting of two enormous domes (i.e. giant greenhouses) where you can see plants and trees from all over the world.

UNIT 5 Tammy

1. Pre-Listening Comprehension

Tammy grew up in Canada but left in her 20s. She now works as a theatre sister and lives in east London, but she has retained her Canadian accent.

Normalisation

This exercise is designed to help you get used to Tammy's voice. Before you listen, try to predict which words, or which types of words (nouns, adjectives, prepositions, parts of verbs, etc.) will fit in the gaps. Then listen and check your answers.

1. Chilliwack is a very small _____ outside Vancouver.
2. It's surrounded by _____, _____ and lakes.
3. It's a very pretty _____ community.
4. Chilliwack is about _____ miles from Vancouver.

2. Listening Comprehension

Gap-fill

Before you listen, try to predict which words, or which types of words will fit in the gaps. Then listen and check your answers.

1. Tammy says Vancouver is a really pretty _____.
2. It's surrounded by _____.
3. It overlooks the _____ and the bay.
4. The University of _____ Columbia is on a peninsula.
5. English Bay is where all the _____ wait to come into the _____.
6. Vancouver has some beautiful _____.
7. The Lion's Gate Bridge begins in Stanley _____.
8. This is in the _____ of Vancouver.
9. The Lion's Gate Bridge ends on the _____ Shore.
10. All the _____ people live there in their big, fancy _____.
11. There are two ski _____ in Vancouver: The Cypress Bowl and Grouse Mountain.
12. They have _____ skiing there all _____.
13. The oldest part of Vancouver is called _____.
14. The oldest _____ in Vancouver is about _____ years old.

A Extension exercise

Fill in the blanks in these new sentences with words you heard during Tammy's interview.

> called   grew   heart   outside   park
> rich   small   wait   winter

1. What's your cat _____?
2. Shall I wait _____ in the car?
3. My father _____ up in Southampton, but he moved to Bristol when he was 18.
4. Could I just have a _____ piece of cake, please? I'm not very hungry.
5. Can you _____ for me? I just need to change my shoes.
6. There's a little _____ near us where the kids play football on Saturdays.
7. You know what they say — cold hands, warm _____!
8. They're not _____, but they have enough money to live comfortably.
9. We had loads of snow last _____.

B Prepositions and adverbs

Put the correct preposition or adverb in the gaps. They are all taken from the interview. Some of them are used twice.

> across   as   at   by   from   in   of   up

1. I think children grow _____ too quickly these days.
2. They live in a little village surrounded _____ hills.
3. Why don't you come _____ out of the cold?
4. How long does it take you to get home _____ work?
5. She's got a wonderful apartment _____ the centre of Washington DC.
6. If you stand in our kitchen you get a beautiful view _____ to the other side of the valley.
7. Do you get lots _____ rain here in winter?
8. This restaurant is just _____ nice as the Peking Chef and it's half _____ expensive.
9. I left Martin _____ home because he isn't feeling _____ all well.

Part 1   (18")

I: Um, where in Canada did you grow up?

T: I grew up in a place called Chilliwack – a very small town outside of Vancouver, **(1) surrounded by mountains**, rivers and lakes. Very pretty. Farming community.

I: Right. Er, how close was it to Vancouver?

T: About 65 miles.

Part 2   (1'27")

I: Can you tell me about Vancouver?

T: It's a really pretty city. It's surrounded by mountains. **(2) It's overlooking the ocean** and **(3) the bay**. Er, the University of British Columbia is actually on **(4) a peninsula** that overlooks the ocean. And then there's a place called English Bay, which is where all the ships wait to come in to the harbour. Um, they've got some beautiful, beautiful bridges. The er, Lion's Gate Bridge which takes you from Stanley Park, which is a large park **(5) in the heart of**

Vancouver across to **(6) the North Shore**, which is where all the rich people live **(7) in their big, fancy houses**. Um, there's two ski hills in Vancouver, one Cypress Bowl and one called Grouse Mountain and they have night skiing there all winter. And they, I think they do man-made snow and so on, but it's, it's there. Um, it's just a really pretty city. It's got lots of **(8) arts and crafts** and things to do and see.

I: Is it um, very old?

T: Er, not as old as er, you'd think. It's not very old at all. It . . . I would say hundred and something. It's not very old at all.

I: Does, does it have an old part of the town?

T: Um, it's got a place called Gastown, which has now become a very touristy area. And that was the original . . . one of the original places. The oldest hotel in there is Hotel Vancouver and that's only about 60, 70, no, 70? About 70 years old, so it's not that old itself, so that's the one that was built first, so . . .

5. Words and Phrases

1 **surrounded by mountains** – there are mountains all around it
2 **It's overlooking the ocean** – from the city you get a good view of the ocean
3 **the bay** – A bay is part of the coast where the land curves in a semi-circle.
4 **a peninsula** – a long piece of land which sticks out into the ocean
5 **in the heart of Vancouver** – in the centre of Vancouver
6 **the North Shore** – A shore is land at the edge of an ocean, lake or wide river.
7 **in their big, fancy houses** – in their large, expensive houses
8 **arts and crafts** – things made by hand